T0304403

HOW TO EXTERMINATE THE BLACK WOMAN

MONICA PRINCE

HOW TO EXTERMINATE THE BLACK WOMAN

PRODUCTION HISTORY

How to Exterminate the Black Woman received its first staged reading at the 40W Theatre in Lakewood, CO as part of the Vintage Theatre's contribution to the International Women's Voices Theatre Festival on January 21, 2018. Special thanks to Margaret Norwood for rescuing this show from the reject pile and directing it with such care and love.

ANGELA & DANCER VOICES.............KIMBERLY SAVAGE-DAWKINS
SILENCE...STEPHANIE HANCOCK
FURY...DR. YVONNE HENDERSON
FEAR...OD DUHU
LOSS...................................ADRIENNE MARTIN-FULLWOOD
EXPECTATION...SHERYL MCCALLUM
NEW...TINY ASHANTIATRENT

How to Exterminate the Black Woman received its first full-length production at Susquehanna University in Selinsgrove, PA on April 13-14, 2018. It was directed by Monica Prince, stage managed by Tajinnea Wilson and Sydni Holloway, and choreographed by Ashley Ward. All lights and sound were done by Tajinnea Wilson, and props were supplied by Monica Prince, except the gun, which came from the Susquehanna University Department of Theatre.

ANGELA.................MADAME SHANON-IMANI BENJAMIN THE FIRST
SILENCE..KARA LITTLE
FURY...REGINE TOMLIN
FEAR...RAVÉN-DAJON COLEMAN
LOSS...PRECIOUS EMMANUEL
                                                           JESSICA NIRVANA RAM
EXPECTATION...TOLULOPE ILORI
NEW...SHANEEKA EMILE
DANCERS...RONNELL HODGES
                                                           CHRISTINA JOELL
                                                           ASHLEY WARD
                                                           JAHMIR WILSON

POEMS BY TITLE

*Come celebrate with me that everyday
something has tried to kill me
and has failed.*
—Lucille Clifton

Lights up. Downstage right stands a coatrack covered in colorful scarves. Each peg has one colored scarf corresponding to the women: green, red, purple, silver, yellow, and blue. Under the coatrack is a lock box that sits unlocked. Otherwise, stage is bare. Curtain opens with Angela standing center upstage alone, dressed in brown. She dances while she recites.

ANGELA
Beloved, you will survive this.
Every day feels like a struggle,
and not just because you are Black
in a nation that prefers you underground.
You are not underfoot, not underwater, though
it may be hard to breathe in the mornings.
No, you'll never be an early riser,
beloved, so when you must wake at dawn,
do it. Make French toast and eat slowly.
Do yoga facing any open window,
because frequently, you won't know
your way home. You won't stop loving
with your whole body, so only love people
just like you. Or at least learn selectivity,
how to identify a train wreck miles
in advance. A man will swallow you—
let him. Another will try—become ghost pepper,
steel wool, a pill too large to take at once.
You are too large to take at once. Your skin
won't break to reveal your squishy heart. Say yes
when asked to use your voice as a weapon.
Say yes when asked if you deserve a country
you built. Say yes when he asks you
to marry him. But don't marry him.
Don't exist only as adjacent to a lover
who will leave, be taken from you.
Remember, beloved: you are unlit candle,
unlocked door, razor blade freshly sharpened.

You won't love any less, but your blood
will stay this hot. If no one will tell you, beloved,
listen now: your love won't save anyone.
But dammit—try anyway.
If anything, save yourself. If nothing,
then yes, nothing.

Angela returns to center downstage. A
other women enter and file in behin
Angela in a single file line, standi
up straight, staring ahead. They rema
still. Angela starts to physically convuls
as if her body is breaking into piece.
She finally faints. The women rema
still for a beat. Slowly, Fear, dressed
green, helps Angela up and they spin
the furthest point stage right. Fear sta
there but Angela starts to faint agai
Fury, dressed in red, goes to her, an
they spin to the furthest point stage lef
Angela tires again and New, dresse
in purple, takes her and spins to th
space beside Fear. Angela weakens an
Silence, dressed in silver, spins her to th
space beside Fury. Angela weakens an
Expectation, dressed in yellow, spin
her to the space beside New. Finall
Angela falls to the ground. Loss, dresse
in blue, helps Angela up, spins her o
stage left, and takes her place betwee
Expectation and Silence. All si
women stare straight ahead. They do n
move during the poem.

ALL
When asked about power, I'll tell them—

FEAR
My mother said Black women live in fear,

NEW
anxious. Born that way. Brand new

EXPECTATION
bodies full of panic, constantly expecting

LOSS
the worst, never taught differently. Losing

SILENCE
such vigilance begets our death, so we stay silent,

FURY
quiet as it's kept, nursing our fury,
hoping it doesn't kill us first. Hell hath no fury

FEAR
like a grieving woman, paralyzed by her fear

NEW
of entombing her own child, maybe herself. The news

EXPECTATION
uses Black bodies as jokes, target practice. You expect

LOSS
our hands to track every ~~hash tag~~ name we've lost?

SILENCE
See us, broken in half, mouths open in silent
wail. You want us to go away, want to silence

FURY
our screaming bloodlines, our vocal chords stretched furious.

FEAR
Will you run when we become fire? Learn to fear

NEW

flame like we've learned about rope? It's a new

EXPECTATION

season to murder us, display on a wall the unexpected

LOSS

trophy for only recognizing loss
when it destroys you. Here we separate, lose

SILENCE

the parts of us born from complacency and silence.

FURY

Find us reborn, boiling our fury

FEAR

until we turn steel, turn threat. We fearless

NEW

women know truths, what novels

EXPECTATION

are birthed in back rooms. We know what to expect:
tension is our territory. Expectation

LOSS

of rebellion should keep you awake. The loss

SILENCE

of home, blood, family. Imagine the silence

FURY

when we rise, glorious, dressed in the magic of this fury

FEAR

you tried to beat out of us, fearful

NEW
of the day we'd wake up and claim our new
names. Pay attention to this new

EXPECTATION
insurrection. Do not cower here, expecting

LOSS
ancestral amnesia. We the bereaved, mourning the loss

SILENCE
of too many loved ones buried in silence,

FURY
white supremacy battled in the dark. We link fury

FEAR
with resolve, welcome cold morning without fear.

Beat.

ALL
My mother said:

SILENCE
accept silence,

FURY
exorcise fury,

FEAR and LOSS
loosen fear.

NEW
Our new hearts cannot.

ALL
Here's a secret:

EXPECTATION
no one ever expects reckoning to be a Black girl.

All women take a breath togethe.
Dancer enters, standing downstag
half-facing the women

DANCER
Sisters, if no one else will—
say her name.

FEAR
Fear.

NEW
New.

EXPECTATION
Expectation.

LOSS
Loss.

SILENCE
Silence.

FURY
Fury.

All exit stage except Silence and New
New looks around, confused as to
why everyone is leaving. Silence doesn'
acknowledge her and New leaves afte.
a beat, determined to figure out what'.
happening

SILENCE

The only time I heard the open palm
of a man's hand skip town on my sister's cheek,
I was asleep in her new bed. I remember
she didn't cry. The night before, we made
spaghetti with meatballs and a Caesar salad.
I only eat well in her home. We finished
a bottle of wine, watched three hours of television,
and slept in her room with the door locked.
Men have a history of arriving unannounced
in our family: my brother was an accident,
the divorce a surprise, my latest breakup
like a child tossed in the freezing deep end.
I lied earlier—I pretended to sleep
when the front door opened with his key.
She slipped from the covers, wide-eyed,
still. I watched her listen for him—
in the living room, the kitchen, the bathroom.
When he tried the bedroom door,
she didn't flinch when he started shouting
her name, voice tinged with anguish.
She went to him, closing the door
behind her, trying not to wake me.
I didn't hear their conversation, but I heard
the slap, the moment my sister turned
to stone, rooted to the anger of a boy
trying to be grown. *Beat her*, Harpo was advised,
and she'll mind. Not my sister. Women have a history
of brandishing weapons in our family: my mother
hurled a curling iron at my father's skull; my grandmother
aimed a .357 at a burglar caught in her kitchen window;
my wine key is tattooed to my palm.
When I opened the door, I was not surprised to find her
already standing over him, knife in steely grip,
breathing evenly. He cowered, the first real fear
I'd ever seen in him. She spoke like a grave,
deep and unwavering: *Leave*.

Our legacy lives in the steady pulse under
my sister's wrist, thumping a drum we've never
seen—the first time is the last time.
I remember she didn't cry. Or speak of it ever again.

Silence exits

DANCER *(offstage)*
I bet you never knew your mama was a sorcerer.
Said the spell correctly, lit the right candle,
poured her blood into the proper cauldron.
She made you out of stardust.

Fury and two dancers enter. They all roll
out yoga mats. Poem is choreographed
alongside the poses mentioned

FURY
On a particularly bad day,
I must lock myself in my house
and roll out my purple yoga mat. I light candles,
shut the blinds, and start from the beginning:
feet planted at the edge, palms pressed at my heart,
eyes forward, spine straight.
Inhale to the back of my ribcage,
exhale from my core. When I met him, yoga
became a sex strategy, not a mindfulness exercise.
I thought it would make him love me.

We fucked so frequently I spent most of my time
in this position: half-pigeon, one leg extended behind,
one leg bent in front, spine elongated,
hands pressed into the mat. Inhale, exhale.
Always through the nose. He never noticed
how tightly my legs wrapped him. He'd just moan
while I flexed and stretched my hips
in butterfly, fire log, and low lunge.

I should have been in chaturanga, lifting my chest
off the ground in cobra, building strength
in my shoulders and across my ribcage in wheel.
Then I could have survived his body,
stone heavy on mine as I flailed,
screaming, using anything available
to escape. He kissed me hard—
put me in an involuntary bow, my wrists
pulled toward my knees—to keep me quiet.
I forgot all my training—audible gasps, mind racing,
my body zipping down the middle.

If I'd mastered the shoulder stand
or fixed my form in plank, I could have lifted us both
off the bed, flipped him out of me.
But the searing blinded me, choked my screams
against the pillow he held to my face.

After two years of sun salutations, strength building,
and breathing techniques, I end up back on my mat,
reliving my own rape through a vinyāsa,
inhaling as prep, exhaling to exert, moving faster and faster
through the poses, sweating, shaking violently.

In the morning, I untangled myself, fell into child's pose,
chest draped over thighs, arms extended forward,
tears dyeing the carpet while he snored.
I couldn't clear my mind then and I can't do it now,
practicing the wrong self-defense, learning
to concentrate on one spot to maintain balance in tree—
instead of how to eat through cotton pillows
or break a sternum with the force of a well-aimed elbow.
I crave a knife to slide between his ribs,
a pill to drop into his beer, an apology that vanquishes
the nightmares I have whenever I drop my guard.

But really, I will do nothing.
I always do nothing.

17

Instead, I take a shower,
roll out this mat, and slide into the splits
until my thighs sting, until I injure myself, until
the joints pop out of sockets and the ligaments snap
and the sparks send me to blackout
because I started yoga to save myself—not
to become more flexible to abuse,
more prone to relax and not fight back.
I close my eyes. Hands to heart. Namaste.

Fury and dancers exit with yoga mats
Fear enters and sits on the edge of the
stage or in a chair. Dancer enters the
audience and starts talking/stumble
dancing toward the stage, drinking from
a flask. Off stage, dancers call out after
each question, steadily increasing in
volume

DANCER	VOICES
Hey, hey Black girl—	
what do you want to be when you grow up?	Alive.
No, for real—what do you want to be?	Alive.
I thought I wanted to be a dancer.	
Misty Copeland style.	
Maybe a physicist, or a motivational speaker.	
Hey Black girl—what do you want to be	
when you grow up?	Alive.
I'm asking for a friend. (It's really me.)	
Tell me—what do you want to be when you grow up?	Alive.
Black girl—what do you want to be?	Alive.
What do you want to be?	Alive.
What do you want to be?	Alive. Ali
	ALIVE!

Dancer reaches the stage and falls
downstage, resting her head on Fear's
lap. When Fear tells her to stand, she
does and begins to dance.

FEAR

When depression opens your skin one night
by sending you tumbling down a flight of brick stairs,
and blood refuses to stay inside your body
just as you were thinking how much you like it
not on concrete or in the synthetic fibers of your green skirt—
stand up, walk home, and draw a bath. No matter
that you just wanted to leave the bar before
you were too drunk to remember where you lived.
And who can account for high heels
or intoxication or depth perception after midnight
with gin and champagne and maybe a hard cider or two
synchronize swimming in your femoral artery?
It's okay. The blood will clot. The stain will rinse out.
Your hands, in their ever-failing attempt to save you,
now scraped, burning, will heal. And yes,
you too will heal. Alcohol is not medicine.
Loneliness is a scar on your forearm
you can't justify; a bruise on your shin no one
asks about; a candle still burning at 6AM
after falling asleep in the tub.

*Fear goes to the dancer, who ends
somewhere upstage on her knees, hands
out and open as if asking for something.*

Maybe don't end your life on accident.
Go out like a champ. On purpose. In flames.
Your body unrecognizable.

*Fear helps dancer get up and both exit.
Loss enters.*

LOSS

The Black girl in the frame is me—
yellow plaid dress, blue barrettes, eyes asking
a question to your question: *What?*
I smoked cigarettes for six months at eighteen,
and it was exactly what everyone said it would be—

sexy. Each puff an emotion: annoyance,
flirtation, stress, resignation. I never mastered
rings or French exhales through my nose,
but my clouds were stories, invitations,
promises to take you somewhere astonishing.

The second time I was raped, I knew not
to shower but I did. I smoked a whole pack
on the train ride to St. Louis—got off at every stop.
It wasn't the nicotine; it was the need to be
someone not so damaged, unhinged, unsalvageable.
We smokers light up death behind cupped hands
every day, choose to stare it in the eyes, and inhale.

Eight years later, I don't smoke anymore.
The smell makes me gag. But when a man
rubbed one out next to me on the train,
his semen a smoke cloud in my face,
I craved the tar between my teeth. Mouth ajar,
first cigarette out of a fresh pack at my lips,
eyes glazed over, begging,
Please, don't let me be this girl again.

> *Loss exits. Expectation enters. A*
> *masculine presenting dancer enters.*
> *They waltz pausing at the line they sing*
> *together.*

EXPECTATION
My daughter will give her father stress dreams,
wild and vivid ones that recur for months,
long before she's born, while we're still locked
in one another, soldered with sweat, awestruck
at the shiver of love. There, she will be made.
No other space could create her. My daughter
will come to him like the angels met Joseph—
but she won't recite prophecy. Rather: she will sing.
Her voice will vibrate his skull, send sparks over his tongue,

electrify his bones. It will become a cloud,
cracking open like an egg, and it will pour
little luxuries into his hands: rings, tampons,
vinyl recordings of Prince, and finally, her heart.
When he wakes, my hands laced in his hair,
all he'll remember is her song. One line, sung over
and over, halting his breath in his lungs:
You will bury every part of me in boxes you will lose.   *(sings with dancer)*
This will not stop us from making love.

> *Expectation and dancer exit,*
> *Expectation dragging the dancer offstage*
> *somewhat seductively. New enters.*

NEW
I don't know how to make pretty
the barrel of a sniper rifle, blood
staining a white t-shirt, the shock
of stun gun on a slightly curved spine.
How are you still beautiful while I
am so angry? How do I trace shadows
on your face while the world goes up
in flames? Has beauty always been
an illusion? I ask because when I told you
I love you, you said I was beautiful.
When I said *I love you*, you told me,
It'll be okay. It won't. And yet,
I can't stop thinking of your majesty,
how stunning you'll be
when they've killed us all.

> *New stays on stage, staring at her*
> *hands. Expectation enters, smoothing*
> *out her clothes as if she has just hastily*
> *put them back on.*

EXPECTATION
What do you mean? Are you talking about
a man? An ally?

NEW
Yes, an ally.
Someone who's supposed to be on our side.

EXPECTATION
Why is our extinction pretty?

> *New looks at Expectation blankly*
> *then floats into the audience.*
> *House lights come up. All the others*
> *including dancers, enter and float into*
> *the audience. Expectation remains*
> *on stage during her stanza, but then*
> *enters the audience. During the poem*
> *everyone invades the space of the*
> *audience members, intentionally making*
> *them uncomfortable without touching or*
> *speaking to them.*

EXPECTATION
The first time I lived on my own, I rented a home
across the railroad tracks, a clichéd reminder
that I was Black. A man once broke
his morning routine to invade my personal space,
asked my number before my name. I wrote a poem
about it that day. Somehow, that didn't seem real

LOSS
or problematic in comparison to the very real
moment weeks later in my home,
in my bed. A different man used his body to remind
me that it would be easy for him to break
my neck—might as well enjoy it. I crave my own space
now, to walk around naked, hang sonnets

FEAR
from the walls, never mix up the fiction with the poetry
on the bookcase. Every nightmare feels real
until I wake up in bed under sunlight at home.

I rarely fear a man's hand on my throat reminding
my nerves—fight, flight, freeze—but my voice still breaks
under the strain of clutter, not enough space

FURY

for air. Men take up all my space,
spread their knees wide, invade my body of a poem,
get comfortable telling me my fear isn't real.
Not all men slip between those legs I call home
and steal all the reminders
of the girl I was before I met them. Way to break

NEW

the cycle; abuse gets trickier when you can't break
bones. This time, since the space
between my heart and my hips throbs like poetry,
I know my muscle memory is real.
Never mind the difficulty of calling home
to tell my mother everything that reminds

SILENCE

her of me may become a reminder
of how those men altered me. She knows heartbreak
looks just like murder some days, too little space
between kills, only enough breath for a haiku.
I want my mother to know what's real
is how badly I want to come home—

All performers stop moving.

LOSS

but I believe one day, I will never again realize
a rapist's fantasy. I'll break a sestina, remember
the route back home, a space entirely mine.

*Loss remains in the audience, while
everyone but Silence exits. Silence climbs
on stage and sits at the edge. As Loss
speaks, she gravitates closer to the stage.*

LOSS
Ever thought about it?

SILENCE
Thought about what?

LOSS
Killing yourself.

> *Silence says nothing, but stares at Loss*
> *as if she has uncovered a dangerou*
> *secret. Loss reaches Silence on the stage*
> *standing beside her with her arms on th*
> *edge like they are watching a sunset*

LOSS
I made a deal with my body when I was twelve.
If I kill myself, I can't open my skin.
No knives, guns, or external trauma.

SILENCE
Why?

LOSS
I think it's a woman thing, you know.
Can't leave too much of a mess.
Like, I don't want my mama to be Mamie Till-Mobley,
don't want her to have to decide
if she will make me an example.
I'm not…an example.

> *Loss exits. Silence watches her leave*
> *then goes to the coatrack to retrieve a*
> *revolver from the lock box under the*
> *coatrack. She takes it back to her*
> *original position on stage.*

SILENCE
My lover asks if we can get a gun
and I picture a canon in the front window.
For weeks, we've watched fictional criminals
shoot and stab and maim on TV, and I wonder,
does he want to lose an eye?

The truth is guns terrify me, which should not
surprise anyone, especially my lover
who is stunned to hear my fear has not yet split
my body lengthwise. He says, *We need*
to protect ourselves because the end is near,
and I tell him, *The end is always tomorrow.*

I want him to know the revolver is my choice
of weapon should I kill myself. It's romantic.
He doesn't understand—we must bear arms
as our enemies do. But what arms will bear me
if I stamp my temple with that barrel's kiss?

*Silence picks up the gun slowly. She
starts to hyperventilate and panic, but
she appears resolved. She takes a big
breath, presses the barrel of the gun to
her head, and fires. Nothing happens.
She sits with the gun pressed to her
temple, visibly shaking and possibly
crying, for a beat as Loss enters. Loss
sees her and runs to her. She grabs the
gun and holds Silence for a beat, who
keeps crying. A dancer enters, picks up
the gun, and starts to remove Silence
from stage. Silence fights the dancer, to
the point that the dancer must literally
drag Silence off stage.*

SILENCE *(screaming and crying out to Loss)*
What if they kill me first?
What should my mama do with my body?

Silence wails as she is taken from the
stage. Loss watches her leave, then takes
a breath.

LOSS

When they call out *crater, canyon, valley*—they mean me.
At eleven, I visited the Grand Canyon. I didn't know

I was reading my own palm. At eighteen,
I miscarried what I imagined to be a son. Ever since,

I've only wanted daughters. The benefit of being
a dark hole in the ground is absorption,

sudden swallowing of emotions—light and otherwise.
I am not a well or a ground spring or laced with a river.

I do not know how to swim. My walls are so steep
only experienced climbers can scale them.

Jagged surfaces slice open their fingers. Assumed
hand holds easily crumble. When a body passes

through you, it takes everything it can hold
in its barely-existent grasp.

My son took my tolerance for deceit, and any courage
I had to kill myself. I used to let visitors in

unannounced. Helicoptered them to my floor
so they could make love to the view from far below.

I thought sharing myself—selling postcards,
organizing excavations of unseen territory—

would keep me on Earth. It turns out replication,
even accidentally with a man

I will always lazily love—that's how to stay alive.
Losing Dorian turned me from vaporous cloud

26

o meteor to desperate crater sculpting a landscape
behind my mother's house. She doesn't know

her daughter is a graveyard, an altar to almost-children.
I worry the ocean will one day drown this canyon body,

fill every crevasse, submerge any memory
of the little boy I never had.

I wonder—what good is memory
if its only service is to suffocate you?

Loss exits. The dancer who removed Silence
returns with the gun, and places it back in
the box under the coatrack, looking around
to make sure no one sees them.

DANCER
Can you breathe, Black girl?
Do you remember how?

Dancer exits. New enters.
She wears a head scarf.

NEW
The decision to shave off all your hair
will arrive like an ex-lover's apology letter—
unexpected, unsolicited, and necessary. Naturally
you consider the claims that this is what Black
women really look like, that we must grow
out of preconceived notions of whiteness

defining our beauty. Pretty doesn't equal white;
rather, if you were Samson, your power would be your hair,
or a political statement if you were Dr. Davis: the first letter
in your name spelled out in your natural
curls. Look—it is hard to be alive and a woman and Black,
so how dare these bloggers ask you to cut off all this hard-earned growth

27

just to start over again? Never mind that it will grow
back. Never mind that you've known you were not white
since Susan or Karen or Taylor called your braids
niggerish in second grade. Never mind the forced letter
that same child wrote to you apologizing for her natural
state as racist. You don't have to do this. We will not revoke your Black

card if you transition differently or not at all. Blackness
is not so easily discarded. Racist children grow
into racist adults. They pass laws prioritizing white
people, white money, white hair-
styles. They criminalize the language
of your ancestors, convince you your curls are unnatural.

It's up to you if you want to go natural,
show off your fire, give them all this Black
Girl Magic. You'll feel like you're doing this wrong, but growing
is both practice and failure. Some things won't change: white
women will still touch your hair
without permission. They don't understand the love letters

your curl pattern's calligraphy conjures, how the alphabet
reorders itself with every twist, braid, loc. The only way to normalize
your default body is to climb inside it, unfamiliar and bleak
as it may be, and get used to what your face looks like. Growth
begins under the scalp, long before a white
man stole your great-great-grandmother by her roots.

No one wishes for whiteness—rather, just natural power
and privilege. Your Blackness is not a mistake. Compose a letter
to your former self as you cut your hair: it will grow back.

New exits. Fury enters.

FURY
I call you Fury.
Rarely does anger leave my body as tackle,
punch, or drop kick. Angry isn't strong enough

a word for the trembling in these muscles.
I call you Fury for your inspired thoughts
of paring knives opening ribcages,
blood painting the skin in black,
purple, yellow, and blue. Fury
because my marrow screams
and my bones rattle with the echoes.
I call you furious, overwhelmed, exhausted,
sick. When you dance, you turn your spirit
into fuel, turn tragedy into turbulence
that brings down planes of emotional baggage
into seas of acid. You are not weak, Fury.
You are brass knuckles breaking cheekbones
and guilty eye sockets. You are boiling oil
splashed on indecent groins. You are bright sky
after monsoon. You are the monsoon.
You are the forecast and declaration
of emergency. But you are not a problem.
No, Fury, you are the first line of defense
against legislature written in Native blood.
You are the oxygen to a fire started on mourning shores.
I call you Fury because no one takes *sad*
or *tired* seriously. You are the coffin in their conscience,
the noose desperate for a white neck, the gleaming smile
in a Black woman's face after a served deadly dinner.
You must be reckoned with,
not just in the streets of your body's country
but in the veins of your enemies. You are not
poison, glorious Fury—you are salvation.

Fury exits.

DANCERS (*offstage, shouting together or popcorn-style*)
I am not extinct. I am not extinct.
I am not extinct. I am not extinct.
I am not extinct. I am not extinct.

Exterminate us as at your peril.

SILENCE
My matrilineal legacy
begins with a white man, an uninvited guest
in a matriarch's womb, her mouth a shotgun,
her legs railroad barriers. Do not enter. Do not pass
Go.
Do not collect credit for the dark

EXPECTATION
children she bore, too dark
for the house. I don't know if mine is a slave's legacy.
I assume so. These women entertain vaginal guests
to stay alive. If I learn to fire a shotgun
into the groin of an intruder trying to pass
his genes onto my progeny, will I go

SILENCE
to Heaven? Or is Heaven only for women who went
along with it? My body is not dark
enough for an African man to believe my direct legacy
isn't mixed. (That means, to be pretty, white guests
must have entered my chromosomes like shotgun
slugs because only black girls who can pass

EXPECTATION
as white get past
his lips.) This is the part where I undergo
a restructuring, redefining my darkness
as akin to royalty, a legacy
my mother wants me to carry. We all do it, I guess.
But I don't want to uncover a shotgun

SILENCE
in the closet of my lover's heart. One shotgun
house is all we have left of the past
where race meant kingdoms. All gone.

I record names in the family Bible in the dark,
trying to preserve what remains of a legacy
built on resistance and rape. Guess

EXPECTATION
who isn't surprised to come home to impromptu guests
on her porch. It's in my blood, right? To shotgun
strangers either stupid or passionate
enough to try to colonize my womb. I don't want to go
back in time, kill whitey, or redarken
my bloodline. I want instead to fashion a new legacy

out of loaded shotguns aimed at unannounced guests.

SILENCE
I pass my hand over our legacy.

EXPECTATION & SILENCE *(holding hands)*
What name should go below mine in this dark woman's lineage?

> *Silence and Expectation exit,*
> *still holding hands. Fear enters.*

FEAR
In bed, my lover asks what it's like
to sell my body.

Moments like this remind me why
he's my lover,

a man I will spend years,
lifetimes with, if I'm careful.

Moments like this remind me
to be careful.

When money is motivation,
legs open like a well-oiled hinge;

submission is easy.
I want to tell him

sometimes it hurt,
and sometimes it was honest,

but instead, I tell him
all sex is transactional

until you fall in love.
He laughs—how cliché

but cliché comes from truth,
for all its repetition.

When we make love, my body
opens like it's gasping for air:

desperate for him, take me
or I'll die.

I tell him what he doesn't realize
he doesn't want to know, how easy it is

to do it again, to answer ads
and reply to texts, to return

flirtatious solicitation when confronted
in a bar, at the bank,

outside 7-Eleven. He holds me
with tattoo needle hands,

just as desperate, more so,
to claim me as his.

There isn't enough water,
steel wool, or bleach.

Just days on a calendar crossed out,
a running tally of closed borders.

*Fear exits. Feminine presenting dancers
enter at the back of the room, wander
around the audience, talking to each
other.*

DANCER 1
Hey Black girl?

DANCER 2
Yeah?

DANCER 1
Have you called on your magic today?

DANCER 3
Have you remembered what your legacy is for?

DANCER 2
Hey Black girl—

DANCER 4
Get off the floor.

DANCER 3
Stand, beloved.

DANCER 1
Your body is vibrating with power.

DANCER 4
Your ancestors are calling.

DANCER 2
Have you checked in today?

DANCER 4
Where is your excellence?

DANCER 3
Can you reach out?

DANCER 2
Do you need some courage?

ALL DANCERS
Look up.

Dancers all turn to look at the stage.
New enters, holding or wearing
something magical (beads, crystals, etc.)
Dancers sit in the audience.

NEW
In the beginning, I loved with my eyes closed.
Hands folded in prayer, I asked the foremothers
for strength. Open my chest; give me a girl
whose body bleeds with the power
of every woman who ruled before her and knew
the capability of an exposed heartbeat.

And they did. I placed my own heart
into the crib, kissed you, kept the nursery door closed.
My body made babies because my mother
and the ones before her all said, *We bring girls*
to life not to sustain this world, but to enrich it. What power
in your generation, child, to know

the gifts you possess. Here's what I know:
one day, you will consider if breaking your heart
for a child surpasses bringing your legacy to a close.
Not every woman wants to be a mother—
not every goddess crafts excellence into a girl.
And yet, your soul has an ancient power

nstilled in you at birth. I felt your power
in my blood the moment I knew
you would come. I danced to your heartbeat,
poured out wine in your honor, prayed closely
around your promised body. As your mother,
I braided the universe in your hair, baby girl.

You're the reason I believe in invincible Black girls,
why not even bullets can extinguish your power,
why your voice weakens hurricanes. They should know
better than to question the footsteps of your heart.
You are not free until we're all free. And we're close.
I can see it. Can you, my miracle? The original mothers

called for you purposefully. If you become a mother,
pray to them and light candles and sing for a little girl
who dances wildly, who conjures empowering
revolutions with her hips, her outspread fingers. Know
this, child: brilliance is your birthright. Your heart
cries *Queen*, for you are magic, dressed in royal clothes.

This mother delivered a powerful Black girl—you.
I closed my eyes, stopped my heart, and knew:
My baby will change the world.

Dancers climb onto the stage and mark a circle of electric candles and exit. New remains on stage. She goes to the coatrack, takes her colored scarf (purple) and puts it around her shoulders. She walks around the stage, confused, annoyed that Angela is still not here. She shouts for the other women to get on stage and retrieve their scarves. All other women enter, visibly annoyed and reluctant. They also go to the coatrack and remove their respective colored scarves. They grumble and complain the entire time while New shouts at them to come stand near her. They wear the

*scarves in different ways: tied aroun
their necks, thighs, waists, heads, etc
They go to the semi-circle marked b
the dancers and stand behind eac
candle, but their body language show
indignation. New moves firs.*

NEW
Lock the doors.
Close the windows, draw the blinds.
Wear something comfortable.

FURY
Question: can I be naked?

EXPECTATION
You always wanna be naked.

FURY
She *said* comfortable.

NEW *(trying to get everyone to focus)*
Wear whatever you want, but no shoes.
Make a circle of candles.
Call out their powers.

FURY *(reluctantly)*
Red for survival.

SILENCE *(rolling her eyes)*
Silver for protection.

EXPECTATION *(bored)*
Yellow for wisdom.

LOSS *(unconvinced)*
Blue for healing.

FEAR *(annoyed)*
Green for growth.

NEW *(frustrated they aren't taking it seriously)*
And purple for the divine.

Light each one carefully.
Sit inside the circle and cross your legs.

> *All enter the circle and sit however they want in a semi-circle: lying down, legs crossed, legs open, etc., the candles sitting before them.*

EXPECTATION
See? Now you're glad you ain't naked.

FURY
Hush, you wanna see my coochie.

NEW *(trying to get everyone to focus but also visibly frustrated)*
Breathe evenly, slowly.
State your affirmation.

ALL *(reluctantly, not convinced this will even work)*
I am divine. I am transcendent.
My body is sacred ground, vessel, and conduit.
I release all pain within this circle.

NEW
Really, y'all? Come on. This is serious.

> *No one looks at her. They clean their nails, look around, or ignore her out right. New is still hopeful, though getting increasingly pissed.*

Name your pain.

FURY *(bored)*
Fury.

SILENCE *(meekly)*
Silence.

LOSS *(defeated)*
Loss.

EXPECTATION *(tired)*
Expectation.

FEAR *(reluctant)*
Fear.

NEW *(now pissed off)*
Come on, y'all. Try!
Know that the pain does not leave you
if it fuels you. This is not a spell
of relaxation, of comfort, of moving on.
This is a spell of motivation.
Pain is the body's language. It tells you
something is wrong, something is changing,
something is new.

*New rises and goes to Expectatio
With each question, New goes to
different woman and demands they sta
and answer her. She remains pissed
because it fuels her, but as each wom
is confronted, they start to feel someth
change within them, and they stop act
aloof. After New leaves them, they da
and at the end they are all doing the sa
dance together in sy*

NEW *(to Expectation)*
Rise.
What is your pain?

EXPECTATION
Expectation.

NEW
What do you expect?

EXPECTATION
A child I may one day bury. A murderer
walking free. My heart ceasing to beat.

NEW
What will you do?

EXPECTATION
Have this baby anyway. Love them. Teach them
royalty and joy. Hope for the best.

NEW *(to Loss)*
Rise.
What is your pain?

LOSS
Loss.

NEW
What did you lose?

LOSS
My name. It has become a hash tag, a chant,
a trending story. But where is my face?

NEW
What will you do?

LOSS
Pour into my body. Reclaim my name. Draw its letters
in blood and ashes on the city's walls.

NEW *(to Silence)*
Rise.
What is your pain?

SILENCE
Silence.

NEW
What took your voice?

SILENCE
I am helpless. I am alone. What is there to say
that hasn't already been spoken? Who am I to history?

NEW
What will you do?

SILENCE
Speak. Scream. Bellow. Until my voice turns haunt,
turns nightmare, turns empty grave, withered noose, crumbling cross.

NEW *(to Fury)*
Rise.
What is your pain?

FURY
Fury.

NEW
What infuriates you?

FURY
My world is on fire and all anyone can see
are streaks of smoke on my people's skin.

NEW
What will you do?

FURY
Become oxygen, become aluminum.
Be elemental by riot.

NEW *(to Fear)*
Rise.
What is your pain?

FEAR
Fear.

NEW
What are you afraid of?

FEAR
I don't want to learn my life's weight in gold.
What if I'm as grotesque gorgeous as they say?

NEW
What will you do?

FEAR
Sprout wings of silver. Climb the wind
like a ladder. Open every cloud and rinse us clean.

NEW *(finally satisfied)*
Sisters.

> *Women return to the circle, take their candles, and hold them. They speak directly at the audience.*

ALL
I am divine. I am transcendent.
May my pain turn propellant, turn promise.
I am a Black woman—I am the original being.
Souls will rise to join my army.
The war is coming.

NEW
Battle stations.

> *All "blow out" candles and lights blackout.*

*Dancers enter and remove the candles and
magical elements from the stage. Lights
up. Angela returns wearing a black scarf
tied around her waist. The women step
forward in a line. Angela goes to each of them
and takes their hands in love and gratitude
then stands in the window between the two
center women. As each woman exits, they
drape their individual scarves over Angela's
shoulder.*

ANGELA

Everyone knows—starting with a furious
God and ending with white men—silently,   *Silence exits*
colored girls want to go extinct, but I don't. Can't. I lose
track of my own legacy within all the expectation
of dying. Call it resilience, perpetual, an encoded dirge, old and new
trees humming the chorus: *Fear*

not. I'm never supposed to be afraid,
only strong. To kill myself is not a victory; giving in to fury   *Fury exits*
is not success. No joy there. Yet, silently,
the blood pools at the body's back. Another Black girl lost
to the same oppressions and expectations
of grandeur or pain. There's nothing new

about a God waiting for me to lift a gun, open a new
razor, strike a match. I refuse to apologize even if I should. Fear   *Fear exits*
is as natural as melanin. Are my ancestors furious
with me after each failed attempt to end my life? Is their silence
their way of asking me to be a little stronger? Whatever loss
I calculate must remain between my heart and my hips—expecting

death by cop, by brother, by my own colored hands. I am patient
as I try to conjure spells for the new   *New exits*
generation, bodies sewn with sinew from my flesh, fearful
of asking for too much. I am tired of asking for too little, infuriated
that my request for dignity in my death may be silently
denied. I used to believe I could be a witch, stop losing

42

my children and my name in the abyss of incomplete and lost
history. I don't know what you expect   *Expectation exits*
from this Black girl shattered into six parts, what new
lessons you hope to learn about the fear
stamped into my bone marrow. You do not ask what fury
tastes like or how to navigate the pregnant silence

after another of my sisters goes up in flames. You're happy silent,
oblivious, uninformed. But the Black woman stays lost—   *Loss exits*
blamed for her children's condition, her men's incarceration—expecting
a blade or pill or bullet to end her suffering before she can present new
evidence of her worth. My worth. You cover your fear
of my dark magical melanin with ignorance. I mask mine with rage.

> *Angela takes all the scarves from her body*
> *and lays them down in a pile on the stage.*
> *She covers them with her own black scarf*
> *and kneels before the make-shift altar.*

ANGELA
Mix all the colors and expect brown. Add silence, fury, loss,
and fear—get black. Here's the new spell: when they ask
how to exterminate the Black woman—tell them:

> *Angela stands, hands at her side.*

Good. Fucking. Luck.

> *Angela remains on stage, daring the*
> *audience to get rid of her. Lights go down.*

NOTES AND ACKNOWLEDGEMENTS

The choreopoem structure and term comes from Ntozake Shange's *fo colored girls who have considered suicide / when the rainbow is enuf* (1975). I am forever indebted to Shange's work. Rest in Power, poet.

"When Asked About Power, I'll Tell Them—," "Coming Home to My Body," "Big Chop," "Releasing the Slave," "Black Girl Magic: Origin Story," and "How to Exterminate the Black Woman" are sestinas (or broken sestinas) written in honor of the six parts of a Black woman featured in this choreopoem. Thank you to Christopher Diaz and the Write About Now writing community in Houston, TX for reviving this form for me.

"Instructions for Temporary Survival" and "When Asked About Power, I'll Tell Them—" appear in my poetry collection, *Instructions for Temporary Survival* (Red Mountain Press, 2019).

"Instructions for Temporary Survival" is written after Ocean Vuong's poem, "Someday I'll Love Ocean Vuong," after Frank O'Hara.

The line "quite as it's kept" in "When Asked About Power, I'll Tell Them—" comes from Toni Morrison's *The Bluest Eye*, the first book I ever read that made me proud to be a Black girl.

"Legacy" makes a reference to Alice Walker's *The Color Purple*.

"Vinyāsa" appears in my poetry collection, Survival Techniques (CreateSpace, 2013), in a different version.

"Letter to the Other Woman: Lipstick and Eyeliner" is part of my chapbook, *Letters from the Other Woman*, published by Grey Book Press (2018).

"Trauma as a Cigarette" is written in response to Frieke Janssens' art series, *Smoking Children*. It first appeared in *Tammy 9* and again in my collection, *Instructions for Temporary Survival*.

"My Lover Dreams of Our Daughter" takes its title from Natasha Trethewey's poem, "My Mother Dreams of Another Country."

"Pretty" is written after Nikki Giovanni's poem, "For Saundra."

"Coming Home to My Body" and "How to Exterminate the Black Woman" both contain a version of the line "the space between my heart and my hips," which is the controlling metaphor for my show, *Testify: A Choreopoem*, produced by the CutOut Theatre in Brooklyn, NY in December 2015.

"Safety First" references *A Christmas Story*.

"Loss as a Canyon" is featured in *Texas's Best Emerging Writers*, published by Z Publishing (2017).

In "Big Chop," the line "it is hard to be alive and a woman and Black" is a paraphrase of Ntozake Shange's line, "bein alive & bein a woman & bein colored is a metaphysical dilemma/ i havent conquered yet," from her poem, "no more love poems #4," in *for colored girls who have considered suicide / when the rainbow is enuf*.

"Releasing the Slave" is published in *The Ibis Head Review*, volume 3, issue 1 (2018).

"Black Girl Magic: Origin Story" was partially inspired by the hash tag #BlackGirlMagic, the event, Practical Magic Live 2017, and ChukwuFumnanya Egbune Camara. It first appeared in *The Same* and later in my collection, *Instructions for Temporary Survival*.

"Battle Stations" is for Kristyn Bridges, Christian Jude, Bekah Lauer, Kathryn Nembhard, and Sable Sanders. Without these women, there would be no choreopoem.

Every mother referenced in this show is mine, Judy Angela Prince, with eternal gratitude.